FEARLESS

UNLEASHING GOD'S FIERCE LOVE IN YOUR WORLD

STUDENT DEVOTIONAL IN EPHESIANS

GREG STIER

DARE 2 SHARE

FEARLESS

A D2S Publishing book
PO Box 745323
Arvada, CO 80006

This devotional may be used independently from or in conjunction with the 4 week youth group curriculum *Fearless*.

Editor: Jane Dratz

Stier, Greg
Fearless: unleashing God's fierce love in your world
ISBN: 978-0-9725507-3-4
Library of Congress Control Number:
Printed in the United States of America
1 2 3 4 5 6 7 8 9 / 15 14 13 12 11 10 09

To Ralph "Yankee" Arnold,
the pastor who showed me how to be
fearless when sharing the gospel.

TABLE OF CONTENTS

INTRODUCTION vii

WEEK 1: EMBRACED
Encircled by God's Fierce, Deep, Lavish Love

1: You! You're the Focus of His Love 2

2: Party Time!. 6

3: Unchained 10

4: Signed, Sealed Delivered 16

5: Juxta-What? 20

6: God's Big Bear Hug. 24

7: Because of His Lavish Love 28

WEEK 2: EMPOWERED
Equipped by the Spirit with a Glorious Inner Strength

8: Career Counseling 32

9: Who, Me? 36

10: Free! Fearless! 40

11: The Cure for Complain-a-mania 42

12: Power Time 46

13: Immense 50

14: Beyond Your Wildest Dreams. 54

WEEK 3: ENGAGED
Living a Life of Love

15: Love Like That! 58

16: Live and Love Before a Watching World 64

17: Don't Be a User. 68

18: Hijacked?!?. 72

19: Carpe Diem. 76

20: Out of Your Coffin!. 80

21: Drinking Songs 84

WEEK 4: EMBOLDENED
Fearlessly Stand and Be Counted

22: Strength Training 88

23: Doubt and Guilt: Send 'em Running for the Hills. . . . 92

24: Let's Roll! 96

25: Gear Up 100

26: Your Dusty Bazooka 104

27: OMG! What Should I Say? 108

28: Fearless! Come What May.... 112

Endnotes 117

INTRODUCTION

We live in a world that longs for love, but often looks for it in all the wrong places.

Many young people try to fill the longing in their heart and the hole in their soul by chasing after pleasure, popularity, partying, possessions, porn and a profusion of other pointless pastimes. When all along, our great God is standing with His arms outstretched, longing for each of us to simply walk into the embrace of His extravagant, unconditional, irrevocable, fierce love.

Because only He can fill the God-shaped hole in our souls.

And when He does, WATCH OUT!

When God embraces you in His lavish love, and you truly let it seep down into the deepest parts of your soul, something amazing happens. Out of the overflow of His great love for you and through the power of His Spirit at work in and through you, you'll find yourself boldly compelled to live for Jesus, and longing to bring others along with you on this amazing journey.

Because once you embrace grace and let grace embrace you, you WANT to serve Christ! Not because you have to, but because you want to. And once you tap into the power of the Holy Spirit, you'll find a power you never knew you had that will help you be bold and fearless as you live for Him and unleash His love in your world.

That's really the essence of what the book of Ephesians is all about: God's love and our response.

What does this look like in practical, everyday life? Well, it will look different for you personally than it will for me. That's part of what's so amazing about our God. He's King of the Universe, and yet He's personal. His relationship with each of us is uniquely fitted to our personality, talents, needs, emotional baggage and circumstances.

These 28 days of daily devotions in the book of Ephesians are designed to help you grow in your understanding of God's love, and help you unpack how you might unleash that love in your own world. We'll be focusing on selected passages that will help us explore the following four themes:

1. **EMBRACED…** Encircled by God's Fierce, Deep, Lavish Love

2. **EMPOWERED…** Equipped by the Spirit with a Glorious Inner Strength

3. **ENGAGED…** Living a Life of Love

4. **EMBOLDENED…** Fearlessly Stand and Be Counted

Get ready to be encircled by the lavish love of your heavenly Father, empowered by His Spirit, enlisted into a life of love and emboldened to fearlessly live for Him and share His message of grace!

A Word about the Bible Translations Used in this Devotional

During weeks one through three of this devo, I chose to draw upon *The Message* paraphrase for each daily Bible reading. *The Message* is a contemporary paraphrase that brings a modern language perspective to the Bible's timeless truths. Its imagery and wording in the early chapters of Ephesians beautifully capture the essence of God's lavish love for us and our grateful response back to Him.

In week four, however, when it was time to unpack the "armor of God" found in Ephesians 6, I chose to use the *New International Version* (NIV), because this is the translation that I memorized this incredibly descriptive passage from in my younger days, and the NIV richly depicts this amazing spiritual armor that God's graciously provided for our protection.

On occasion throughout this devo, I also used the *New Living Translation* (NLT), when I thought that it best captured the meaning of a particular verse or passage for you, the reader.

Since I'm the author, I felt free to move between these translations or the paraphrase. But since you're the reader, I hope you'll feel free to crack open you own personal favorite version of the Bible, and study each day's verses in the one that suits you best!

LESS

You! You're the Focus of His Love

1

Ephesians 1:4

Long before he [God] laid down earth's foundations, he had us in mind, had settled on us as the focus of his love, to be made whole and holy by his love.

Explore

God's extravagant, lavish love for you is deep and wide, fierce and focused, unconditional and irrevocable.

It almost seems too good to be true, doesn't it? That the mighty God who laid the foundations of the earth longs to laser-focus a love like that into your soul, and make you *"whole and holy by his love."*

Do you really believe that God loves you like that, warts and all? Not because you've "earned" it by trying to be good or do good, but just because **He is** the very definition of love itself.

God's love is a free gift, extended to you no matter how battered, broken, bad and blamable you might feel. *"God showed his great love for us by sending Christ to die for us while we were still sinners"* (Romans 5:8, NLT).

We don't have to clean up our act for God to encircle us with His deep, fierce, lavish love.

In fact, it's His crazy, **amazing** love that has the power to heal our brokenness and bring us into a rich, personal relationship with Him. We're made *"whole and holy,"* not by what we do, but by what He's done for us.

I want to be embraced by a love like that. **Don't you?**

☀ Encounter

Mere words are inadequate to capture the expanse of God's love for you. Still, we have to start somewhere. The key is to move the words off the page into your soul.

So ask God through His indwelling Holy Spirit to help you, and one-by-one, pull each of the following six words that describe God's love for you into your heart and soul. Think for awhile about each word individually, hold it tight and let it soak into your soul. Then jot down a short phrase about what it means to you personally.

GOD'S LOVE FOR ME IS...

Lavish

He wanted us to enter into the celebration of his lavish gift-giving by the hand of his beloved Son *(Ephesians 1:6)*.

IMMENSE

For his unfailing love toward those who fear him is as great as the height of the heavens above the earth *(Psalm 103:11, NLT)*.

Fierce

"For God loved the world so much that he gave his one and only Son, so that everyone who believes in him will not perish but have eternal life" *(John 3:16, NLT)*.

FOCUSED

Long before he [God] laid down earth's foundations, he had us in mind, had settled on us as the focus of his love, to be made whole and holy by his love *(Ephesians 1:4)*.

UNCONDITIONAL

He has removed our sins as far from us as the east is from the west *(Psalm 103:12, NLT)*.

IRREVOCABLE

For God has said, "I will never fail you. I will never abandon you" *(Hebrews 13:5b, NLT)*.

🗨 Engage

Talk to God right now, and ask Him to show you more of Himself across the next 28 days of these *Fearless* devo readings. Invite Him to guide you into a deeper, richer place with Him. Ask Him to show you, day-by-day, what it looks like in **YOUR** life to fearlessly experience and extend His deep, fierce, lavish love more and more fully.

Party Time!

2

Ephesians 1:5-6

Long, long ago he [God] decided to adopt us into his family through Jesus Christ. (What pleasure he took in planning this!) He wanted us to enter into the celebration of his lavish gift-giving by the hand of his beloved Son.

🧭 Explore

Imagine with me what it would be like to grow up in a war-torn, poverty-stricken country like Syria or South Sudan. You're hungry 24-7. Gunfire and violence echo endlessly around you, and inside your head. When illness strikes, there's no doctor or medicine. Now imagine that both your parents have been killed. You're orphaned and homeless, out on the streets fending for yourself. Your life is a desperate struggle in a hostile, dangerous world.

You'd feel pretty helpless and hopeless, wouldn't you?

BUT ONE DAY SOMETHING INCREDIBLE HAPPENS!

Brad Pitt and Angelina Jolie swoop in and adopt you! You go from poverty to plenty— beyond your wildest dreams. From an abandoned orphan on the gritty streets, to a cherished member of a loving family, full of other adopted kids who've been rescued from desperate circumstances, too. Your new parents take great pleasure in showering you with lavish gifts—and not just "stuff," but more importantly, love, care and emotional security. You've gone from rags to riches!

WOULD YOU FEEL LIKE CELEBRATING? YES!!!

☀ Encounter

Did you know that something even more miraculous than being adopted into the Jolie-Pitt family has actually happened to you as a follower of Jesus?

Before you accepted Jesus' free gift of salvation, spiritually you were like a poverty-stricken orphan, hungry, battered and homeless, wandering in a broken, fallen world, lost and separated from God. But because of Jesus' work on the cross, the way was opened for you to be adopted into God's family! John 1:12 puts it like this: *"But to all who believed him and accepted him, he gave the right to become children of God* (NLT).

In fact, the Bible tells us **we can approach God as *Abba***, which in the language of that day was the equivalent of "Daddy" (Galatians 4:6). Isn't it amazing that the God of the Universe wants you to call him Daddy?

As His cherished child, your *Abba*-Daddy takes great pleasure in lavishing all sorts of incredible gifts on you: His love and forgiveness, a restored personal relationship with Him through Jesus, a meaningful, abundant life here and now as you walk with Him, and eternal life in the forever after of the ultimate party scene—heaven.

Engage

Sometimes, Christians act like they've been baptized in lemon juice—all sour, scowly and grumpy, when, instead, we should be the most joyful people on the planet!

Does God's love for you make you feel like celebrating? It should! True joy naturally flows out of a grateful heart. And we have a lot to be grateful to God for. Take a few minutes right now, and give God a big, huge THANK YOU for adopting you into His family, and lavishly giving you the incredible spiritual gifts that are yours in Christ.

Then, because of what your *Abba*-Daddy has done for you, look for ways to share your party spirit today. Smile, laugh, be kind and generous, help someone in need, or whatever other creative idea God puts on your heart.

Every day should be a party when God is our loving Daddy!

Unchained 3

Ephesians 1:7-8
Because of the sacrifice of the Messiah, his blood poured out on the altar of the Cross, we're a free people—free of penalties and punishments chalked up by all our misdeeds.
And not just barely free, either. Abundantly free!

Explore

Say you really messed up. Say you got busted for movie piracy big time, and the movers and shakers in the movie industries are determined to make an example of you. They are out for blood, and looking for the maximum fines—$100,000 a pop for each violation, or prison time if you can't pay the fines. And your download record shows multiple violations. You are in BIG trouble.

Hauled into court, you stand before the judge.

GUILTY. GUILTY. GUILTY. GUILTY. GUILTY. GUILTY. GU
GUILTY. GUILTY. GUILTY. GUILTY. GUILTY. GUILTY. GU
GUILTY. GUILTY. GUILTY. **GUILTY.** GUILTY. GUILTY. GU

GUILTY. **GUILTY.** GUILT

ILTY. **GUILTY.** GU

TY. **GUILTY...**

on every single count, he finds you GUILTY
and assesses you a steep fine for each violation, upholding the letter of the law.

Oh no, I can never pay my fines, you think. So the judge is going to lock me away for years. I'm scared to death. The prison thugs will beat me to a pulp. I'll never survive. My life is ruined.

But then something remarkable happens.

After issuing the verdict, the judge steps down from the bench, and takes off his robe. He pulls out his checkbook, writes a check for the full amount of your fines, and announces to the court that your penalty is "paid in full."

Why would the judge pay out hundreds of thousands of dollars to pay your penalty for you? Because the judge happens to be your father, and he loves you unconditionally.

You're free! Free from punishment, free from fear.

☀ Encounter

Like the father in this story, in the spiritual realm, God has stepped in, and paid the penalty for all your misdeeds and mess-ups—past, present and future. He wrote a check with His life when He died on the cross and paid for your sin.

Why? Because He loves you.

If you've never trusted Christ, or aren't totally sure that you have received this free gift of salvation, check out the GOSPEL box on page 15. It will help you understand and embrace this gift that sets you free!

And if you have trusted in Christ, the Bible declares you not just barely free, but totally free! *"Abundantly free!"*

Do you feel totally free from the burden of guilt and shame? Many Christians continue to struggle with a nagging voice inside their head, telling them that they'll never be good enough for God to really love them and totally forgive them. Do you?

This voice could be the evil one—the Bible calls him "the Accuser" and "the father of lies." Or it could be your own stricken conscience, reminding you of some sin that packs a wallop of shame.

Yet God tells you differently.

Engage

Read each of the following Bible verses, and write a response to God about how each of these promises make you feel.

1 John 1:9 *If we confess our sins, He is faithful and just and will forgive us our sins and purify us from all unrighteousness* (NIV).

Romans 8:1 *So now there is no condemnation for those who belong to Christ Jesus* (NLT).

Micah 7:19 *Once again you will have compassion on us. You will trample our sins under your feet and throw them into the depths of the ocean!* (NLT).

Do you know someone else who struggles with feeling unlovable? Maybe they wrestle with discouragement, self-injury or depression. Pray for them today, and ask God to show you a way to share His love with them, and point them toward the freedom that can be found in Jesus.

The Gospel

The Gospel means "good news," and is explained by the following six key truths.

God created us to be with Him. (Genesis 1-2)

Our sins separate us from God. (Genesis 3)

Sins cannot be removed by good deeds. (Genesis 4 – Malachi 4)

Paying the price for sin, Jesus died and rose again. (Matthew – Luke)

Everyone who trusts in Him alone has eternal life. (John)

Life with Jesus starts now and lasts forever. (Acts - Revelation)

Is there anything holding you back from putting your faith in Jesus right now to give you eternal life? The moment you trust in Jesus, you enter into an eternal relationship with God. Your life will never be the same. Both now and for all eternity.

While saying a prayer isn't what gets you into a relationship with God, it is a way for you to express your newfound faith in Jesus. You might pray something like this...

"Dear God, I know that my sins have broken my relationship with You, and that nothing I could do could ever change that. But right now, I believe that Jesus died in my place, and rose again from the dead. I trust in Him to forgive me for my sins. Through faith in Him, I am entering an eternal relationship with You. Thank You for this free gift! Amen."

For more information, go to www.somethingamazing.net.

Signed, Sealed, Delivered

Ephesians 1:13-14

It's in Christ that you, once you heard the truth and believed it (this Message of your salvation), found yourselves home free— signed, sealed, and delivered by the Holy Spirit. This signet from God is the first installment on what's coming, a reminder that we'll get everything God has planned for us, a praising and glorious life.

Explore

Imagine applying to a university, and having the Admissions Office call to inform you that you're missing one important form that needs your principal's signature in order to be considered for a big scholarship. But the deadline's tomorrow. So you rush to get the form printed, filled out and signed. You get a large FedEx envelope, put the form inside it, peel off the little tape thing that covers the sticky stuff on the lip of the letter, seal it and pay the right amount of postage you need to get it to its final destination overnight. Finally, you send it with the full expectation of it getting to where it needs to go.

But once you send the letter, it's out of your hands. It probably will make it to the desired destination, but there are no guarantees. It could get lost in the mail. The FedEx plane carrying it could crash.

That's where salvation is different.

God *signs* the letter,

the Holy Spirit SEALS it and

Jesus *delivers* you to
your final destination.

And Jesus **never** loses his mail.

Encounter

What does it actually look like for you to be *"sealed by the Holy Spirit"*? Great question! Let's take a quick look at just a few of the things Scripture tells us about the Third Person of the Trinity's role in your life.

HE GIVES YOU NEW LIFE. *"He saved us, not because of the righteous things we had done, but because of his mercy. He washed away our sins, giving us a new birth and new life through the Holy Spirit"* (Titus 3:5, NLT).

HE SEALS YOU AS BELONGING TO GOD. *"[God] set his seal of ownership on us, and put his Spirit in our hearts as a deposit, guaranteeing what is to come"* (2 Corinthians 1:22, NIV).

HE LIVES INSIDE YOU. *"Don't you realize that your body is the temple of the Holy Spirit, who lives in you and was given to you by God?"* (1 Corinthians 6:19a, NLT).

HE TEACHES YOU TRUTH. *"But the Advocate, the Holy Spirit, whom the Father will send in my name, will teach you all things and will remind you of everything I have said to you"* (John 14:26, NIV).

HE EMPOWERS YOU TO BATTLE SIN. *"And because you belong to him, the power of the life-giving Spirit has freed you from the power of sin that leads to death"* (Romans 8:2, NLT).

HE GIVES YOU SUPERNATURAL GIFTS TO SERVE OTHERS. *"It is the one and only Spirit who distributes all these gifts. He alone decides which gift each person should have"* (1 Corinthians 12:11, NLT).

🗩 Engage

The Holy Spirit's presence in your life means that you are never alone! Because the Spirit lives inside you, even if you feel alone... you are not.

Take a moment right now, and...

Thank the Spirit for living inside you and for all He's at work doing in your life.

Invite Him to empower you today.

Listen for His promptings throughout your day and step into the **opportunities** He sends your way to share God's light and love with others.

Juxta-What? 5

Ephesians 1:17-21

*I ask—ask the God of our Master, Jesus Christ, the God of glory—
to make you intelligent and discerning in knowing him personally,
your eyes focused and clear, so that you can see exactly what it is
he is calling you to do, grasp the immensity of this glorious way of
life he has for his followers, oh, the utter extravagance of his work
in us who trust him—endless energy, boundless strength!*

*All this energy issues from Christ: God raised him from death and
set him on a throne in deep heaven, in charge of running the
universe, everything from galaxies to governments, no name and
no power exempt from his rule. And not just for the time being, but
forever. He is in charge of it all, has the final word on everything.*

◈ Explore

Reread the Bible passage on page 20, but this time look for the two mind-bending truths juxtaposed within it.

FYI, **juxtaposed** is just a big word for when two contrasting observations sit side-by-side.

SIDE -BY- SIDE

Do you see them? Paul, the writer of Ephesians, is...

1. Praying that his readers (like you) would **know God personally**, so you can see exactly what God is calling **you** to do as His follower.

2. Declaring that Christ is in charge of running the universe—and just for some context, scientists estimate that there may be as many as 500 billion galaxies in the universe![1] That's our Milky Way galaxy multiplied by 500,000,000,000! Jesus is in charge of everything!

In our finite little brains, the contrast of those two truths is strikingly astounding: God runs the universe. God wants a personal relationship with you.

☼ Encounter

Just look at the power words used in the passage: *immensity, utter extravagance, endless energy, boundless strength*. Our God is infinitely powerful.

Yet while God's large and in charge, we're invited to connect with Him on a personal level. We do this through prayer, worship, reading His Word and listening to His Spirit guide us. Why? So that we can receive the wisdom, discernment, focus and clarity we need as we follow Him.

See what I mean about mind-bending?

A famous old church dude named Charles Spurgeon once compared our efforts to understand the infinite God to a gnat trying to drink in the ocean.

Or I've heard it described like this. Here I am, and my puny brain can barely grasp algebra, yet trying to comprehend God and His ways is far, far beyond Calculus, Differential Equations and Chaos Theory.

I offer these comparisons, not because we shouldn't strive to know God more and more, but because we must remember to approach Him with BOTH confidence and humility. We must listen to Him more than we talk, we must search the Scriptures for His truth, we must seek godly counsel from others who follow Him well, and we must yield to His Spirit's guidance in all things.

🗨 Engage

A gnat drinking the ocean…

A math-challenged student trying to understand Differential Equations…

God's large and in charge, and yet we're invited to connect with Him on a personal level. To help cement this incredible, mind-bending truth in your heart, draw a sketch of one of these word pictures that attempts to depict the immensity of our infinite God in comparison to us. Or come up with your own illustration that captures this truth.

God's Big Bear Hug 6

Ephesians 2:4-9

...Immense in mercy and with an incredible love, he embraced us. He took our sin-dead lives and made us alive in Christ. He did all this on his own, with no help from us! Then he picked us up and set us down in highest heaven in company with Jesus, our Messiah.

Now God has us where he wants us, with all the time in this world and the next to shower grace and kindness upon us in Christ Jesus. Saving is all his idea, and all his work. All we do is trust him enough to let him do it. It's God's gift from start to finish! We don't play the major role. If we did, we'd probably go around bragging that we'd done the whole thing! No, we neither make nor save ourselves. God does both the making and saving.

⊘ Explore

Have you ever gone up and embraced someone you love, who has just been devastated by some terrible hurt or personal tragedy? Just encircled them in your arms, and held them tightly in a big bear hug? You want to make everything right for them again, don't you?

This is the image that comes to mind when I read these words: *"...Immense in mercy and with an incredible love, **he embraced us.** He took our sin-dead lives and made us alive in Christ. He did all this on his own, with no help from us!"*

In the spiritual realm, when you put your trust in Jesus, God's grace embraces you and removes the eternal punishment you deserve for your sin. His mercy and grace are boundless—

His MERCY spares you from the penalty you do deserve, and His GRACE blesses you with kindness that you don't deserve.

There's nothing you do to earn this mercy and grace that grants you salvation. His spiritual rescue of you is totally a free gift. *"Saving is all his idea, and all his work. **All we do is trust him enough to let him do it.** It's God's gift from start to finish!"*

But what does "trusting Jesus" really look like?

☀ Encounter

Putting your faith in Jesus literally means that you trust, depend on and rely upon Him fully. This is the same kind of faith you exercise when you plop down on a chair and expect it to hold you up. When you trust in Jesus, you are putting your full weight of dependence on Him, and what He did for you on the cross.

Perhaps you're more familiar with this passage in the NIV translation of the Bible. Here's how Ephesians 2:8-9 reads: *"For it is by grace you have been saved, through faith—and this is not from yourselves, it is the gift of God—not by works, so that no one can boast"* (NIV).

Many people think you can earn your way to heaven by being "good enough," but God says differently. It's very clear here that it's NOT about our good works.

It's not about trying, it's about trust- ing.

🗩 Engage

Read the following verses one more time.

> *Immense in mercy and with an incredible love, he embraced us. He took our sin-dead lives and made us alive in Christ. He did all this on his own, with no help from us!*

Close your eyes,

and **visualize** God embracing you in His incredible love

with a BIG BEAR HUG.

SILENTLY REST in His embrace for a few moments.

Then return His embrace

and tell Him how much you love Him

and how grateful you are

for His MERCY and GRACE.

As you walk through the next 24 hours, give at least three people an encouraging hug (or high five, if you prefer). Let your actions remind you of God's loving embrace of you, and look for ways to share the immensity of His love with those around you.

Because of His Lavish Love

7

Ephesians 2:10

He creates each of us by Christ Jesus to join him in the work he does, the good work he has gotten ready for us to do, work we had better be doing.

Explore

I once had the opportunity to share the gospel with a full-on gang member. He was one big, rough, tough dude. But right there in the food court of a mall in Colorado Springs, he prayed and put his faith in Jesus, accepting His free gift of salvation.

Then I posed this scenario.

"Say I gave you a duffle bag with a million dollars in it, and told you it was a free gift from me to you. What would you do? Would you spit on me or beat me up or walk away?" I asked.

"No," he responded. "I'd thank you and buy you a hamburger." (Remember, we were in a food court.)

"Why? Why would you want to do that?"

"Because I'm thankful for what you've done for me!"

"Exactly!" I said, "Same thing with Jesus. He's given you this amazing gift that's worth even more than a duffle bag with a million dollars. Now it's time to serve Him out of the gratitude of your heart for what He's done for you. Not because you have to, but because you WANT to!"

☀ Encounter

God's extravagant love for you is the pulsing heartbeat of the Bible—His love letter to you. As you've been reading these devos in Ephesians, I hope you're reveling in the embrace of His love, and realizing how very saved, safe and set free you really, truly are in Jesus.

But now we come to another incredibly audacious truth. God is inviting you to *"join Him in the work He does, the good work he has gotten ready for us to do, work we had better be doing."*

The Apostle Paul is not talking here about doing "good works" to earn our way to heaven, or to earn God's love. If you're a believer in Jesus Christ, you are safe and secure in those. In fact, there's nothing you can do to make God love you more. And there's nothing you can do to make God love you less.

No, he's talking here about how *because of* God's

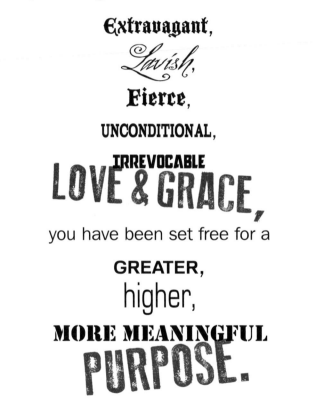

Extravagant,

Lavish,

Fierce,

UNCONDITIONAL,

IRREVOCABLE

LOVE & GRACE,

you have been set free for a

GREATER,

higher,

MORE MEANINGFUL

PURPOSE.

Because once you embrace grace, and let grace embrace you, you WANT to serve Christ!

🗨 Engage

What about you? Are you up for serving Jesus because of all He's done for you? Are you willing *"to join Him in the work He does, the good work he has gotten ready for us to do"*? What is this good work? Well, that's what we'll be exploring in more detail in next week's devo readings—and we'll take a look at how God empowers and equips you as you join Him in His work. But today, let's start with a simple step.

Think a minute about a way you could be of service to someone today in Jesus' name. Here are a few ideas to get your brain churning, but feel free to be creative and come up with your own, if you prefer.

- Listen to someone who's hurting.
- Offer to pray for someone—then do it right then and there.
- Give a compliment.
- Buy someone coffee.
- Sit with a loner at lunch.
- _____
- _____
- _____

Pray about it, settle on one or more, and then go share God's love with someone.

Career Counseling 8

Ephesians 3:7
This is my life work: helping people understand and respond to this Message.

🧭 Explore

Have you ever thought about what you want your "life work" to be? Maybe your mind goes to video game graphic design, business or medicine. The list of possible career paths for earning your way and making a difference in the world is practically endless.

Do you know how the Apostle Paul earned his living? For a big chunk of his life, he was a tentmaker. He travelled a lot, and everywhere he went, back in his day, people needed tents. It was a versatile, mobile occupation, so it was a good fit for him, in terms of earning his room and board as he frequently relocated his base of operations.

But is what we do to earn money for our physical needs, the same thing as our "life work"? Paul didn't think so. He says here in Ephesians 3:7, *"This is my life work: helping people understand and respond to this Message."*

-☼- Encounter

Did you know that as a follower of Jesus, this is your life work too? Jesus' didn't just call "full-time missionaries" to this task; He called every single one of His followers to it! So whether you're a full-time student, car mechanic, or Fortune 500 CEO, this task is at the central core of what every Christian is called to be about every day as you *"join Him in His good work."*

But don't take it from me—or Paul—for that matter. Take a look at what Jesus had to say. Here are a few key Bible verses that bring focus to His work in the world and His invitation for you to join Him in it.

WORK...

- *"The Son of Man came to seek and to save the lost"* (Luke 19:10, NIV).

- *"For God loved the world so much that he gave his one and only Son, so that everyone who believes in him will not perish but have eternal life"* (John 3:16, NLT).

- *"I am the way, the truth, and the life. No one can come to the Father except through me"* (John 14:6, NLT).

INVITATION TO JOIN HIM IN HIS WORK

- *"Come, follow me, and I will show you how to fish for people!"* (Matthew 4:19, NLT).

- *"As the Father sent me, I am sending you"* (John 20:21b).

- *"Therefore, go and make disciples of all the nations, baptizing them in the name of the Father and the Son and the Holy Spirit. Teach these new disciples to obey all the commands I have given you. And be sure of this: I am with you always, even to the end of the age"* (Matthew 28:19-20, NLT).

EMPOWERED 8

Engage

OK. You decide… according to Jesus' own words…

What did He come to earth to do? _____

_____

What is He calling you to do as His follower? _____

_____

Why is sharing His message with others so important? ___

_____

How do you feel about Jesus' calling you to join Him in His work of sharing this Message of love and grace? **Excited? Intimidated? Enthusiastic? Overwhelmed? Fearless? Frightened?** Talk to God right now about it. If you're feeling a bit intimidated, no worries, that just means there's even more room for God to move in and help you share the most important message on the planet with others.

But right now, no matter where you're at with this, write Him a note. He wants you to continually bring your cares, concerns and joys to Him!

Dear God, _____

_____

_____

_____

_____

_____

_____

_____

Who, Me? 9

Ephesians 3:8-10

When it came to presenting the Message to people who had no background in God's way, I was the least qualified of any of the available Christians. God saw to it that I was equipped, but you can be sure that it had nothing to do with my natural abilities. And so here I am, preaching and writing about things that are way over my head, the inexhaustible riches and generosity of Christ. My task is to bring out in the open and make plain what God, who created all this in the first place, has been doing in secret and behind the scenes all along. Through followers of Jesus like yourselves gathered in churches, this extraordinary plan of God is becoming known and talked about even among the angels!

Explore

In *The Lord of the Rings*, Frodo Baggins was a small, unassuming, insignificant hobbit. A most unlikely candidate for the great task of destroying the One Ring, and breaking the hold of the evil power spreading through Middle Earth.

It's easy for us to feel a bit like Frodo when we step up to this grand task of helping others understand and respond to Jesus' gospel message.

Even the great Apostle Paul felt inadequate for the task God had called him to of *"presenting the Message to people who had no background in God's way."*

But take heart! Just like God saw to it that Paul was equipped, He can do the same for you.

☀ Encounter

It's important to remember that God is not asking you to coerce others to put their trust in Jesus. Like Paul, your task is to *"bring out into the open and make plain"* Jesus' gospel message. Your job is to paint a picture of who Jesus is for those who don't know Him, so they can make up their own minds about whether to trust in Him, and receive the free gift of a restored relationship with God.

So how do you go about doing that?

A good place to start is to learn how to explain the gospel in a clear, concise, compelling way. I do this by using the **GOSPEL** acrostic that you may remember seeing in Devo #3. To review, it goes like this:

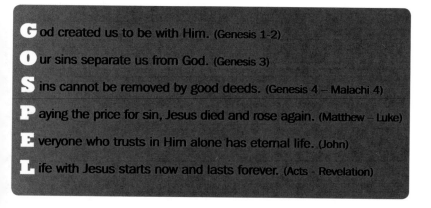

G od created us to be with Him. (Genesis 1-2)

O ur sins separate us from God. (Genesis 3)

S ins cannot be removed by good deeds. (Genesis 4 – Malachi 4)

P aying the price for sin, Jesus died and rose again. (Matthew – Luke)

E veryone who trusts in Him alone has eternal life. (John)

L ife with Jesus starts now and lasts forever. (Acts - Revelation)

EMPOWERED 9

💬 Engage

I know memorizing can be a pain. But I promise you that the more familiar you are with this simple acrostic explanation of the gospel, the more equipped you will feel when God sends an opportunity your way to share Jesus' message with someone.

Keep in mind that the **GOSPEL** acrostic is not designed to be a formula or script that you recite to those who need Jesus. Instead, think of it more as the prep work needed to play a guitar. First, you learn the chords, because they give you the basics you need to be creative and play your own music. In the same way, the **GOSPEL** acrostic provides you the basics you need to share the gospel personally and powerfully in a give-and-take conversation, knowing that you have the basic building blocks you need to clearly communicate the message of the gospel.

If you have a smartphone, go to www.dare2share.org/mobileapp, and download the free app that will help you learn how to use the **GOSPEL** acrostic in your conversations.

If you don't have a smartphone, no big deal. Work on memorizing the acrostic by re-copying it in the following space.

G od _____

O ur _____

S ins _____

P aying _____

E veryone _____

L ife _____

Free! Fearless!

Ephesians 3:11-12

All this is proceeding along lines planned all along by God and then executed in Christ Jesus. When we trust in him, we're free to say whatever needs to be said, bold to go wherever we need to go.

🧭 Explore

Selfies have become an art form. It's fun to snap photos of ourselves with those we love and share them.

But consider this. Before the very foundations of the earth were laid, in His mind, God took a selfie of you and Him together!

Remember the verse we talked about back in Devo #1? Ephesians 1:4 says: *"Long before he laid down earth's foundations, he had us in mind, had settled on us as the focus of his love..."*

How cool is that?!? There's God on the front end of space and time, taking a selfie with you, so to speak! The Bible says that you were in His focus before the world was even created!

☀ Encounter

And now, here in Ephesians 3:12, Paul's reminding us that because of the place we hold in God's heart, and out of the immeasurable love He has for us in Christ, we are "free to say whatever needs to be said" and "bold to go wherever we need to go."

So let's take our selfie illustration a bit further. Are you sharing your selfie of you and God with your friends? Are you showing them a picture of the personal, loving relationship you have with Him?

The Bible says that you were in His focus before the world was even create

🗨 Engage

There's a simple approach I call "Ask – Admire – Admit" that can help you freely and boldly share the gospel. As you begin to initiate spiritual conversations with others, try the following:

ASK questions to understand where they're coming from, and what they believe about God. *"Can you tell me more about Wicca? I'm really not very familiar with it."*

ADMIRE what you can about what they believe. *"I really appreciate how Wiccans embrace the reality of the supernatural."*

ADMIT that the reason you're a Christian is that you're so messed up that you need someone else to rescue you. *"May I share with you more about the One who rescued me?"*

You can watch a video that explains more about how to use this approach at www.dare2share.org/worldviews. Check it out.

Now it's time to step up and be bold. Pray, then try it out. Have an "Ask – Admire – Admit" conversation with a friend who needs Jesus today.

The Cure for Complain-a-mania

11

Ephesians 3:13-15

So don't let my present trouble on your behalf get you down. Be proud! My response is to get down on my knees before the Father, this magnificent Father who parcels out all heaven and earth.

Explore

We live in a culture that loves to complain. Scan your Facebook friends' posts, listen to your peers lunchtime conversations. From siblings to parents to homework to money (or lack thereof), complaining all too frequently becomes our default conversation.

We are late to eat one meal and we complain that we're "starving."

(Seriously, there are people in the world who haven't eaten for days!) Someone makes a snide comment about something we're wearing, and we complain to our parents that they don't give us enough money for clothes. One strict teacher, who actually carries out on her threats to bring us down a grade if we don't turn our papers on time, is suddenly a "horrible teacher."

Let's face it, we're
a BUNCH of
complainiacs.

But now, into our complaining mindset bounces the joy-filled Apostle Paul. *"Don't let my present trouble on your behalf get **you** down,"* he says. What's this "present trouble" Paul's referring to? He's under arrest for spreading the message of Christ.

Most of us would consider prison time for sharing Jesus with others pretty serious trouble. We'd probably dive right into our complain-a-mania mode with anyone and everyone who'd listen!

But think about it... throughout our last 10 days of devos in the book of Ephesians, we've listened in on Paul describing the immense, extravagant love of God and His mighty power to save. Seriously!! Not one word of complaint about how God hasn't sprung him from prison and rescued him out of his present trouble. In fact, in today's passage we see him actually trying to cheer up his readers, telling **them** not to let his present troubles get **them** down. And they're not even the ones in prison!

☀ Encounter

How was Paul able to reconcile the harsh reality of his difficult personal situation with his unquestioning conviction that God is good, loving, merciful and all-powerful?

I believe he had at least two essential tactics for battling complain-a-mania and trusting in God, come what may.

Tactic #1: Contentment in Christ. Regardless of whatever difficulties had blown up in Paul's personal situation, he consistently kept his focus on Christ, and the things that are of eternal significance. Keeping His eyes on Jesus enabled him to look beyond his present troubles, and rest contentedly in his deep, rich, loving relationship with Jesus. In Philippians 4:11-13—which Paul also wrote from prison—he puts it like this:

> *...for I have learned how to be content with whatever I have. I know how to live on almost nothing or with everything. I have learned the secret of living in every situation, whether it is with a full stomach or empty, with plenty or little. For I can do everything through Christ, who gives me strength* (NLT).

Tactic #2: Prayer. Paul took everything to God in prayer. Today's passage is a perfect example. After briefly mentioning his present trouble, he shares his stress reduction strategy:

> *My response* [to my present trouble] *is to get down on my knees before the Father, this magnificent Father who parcels out all heaven and earth.*

He takes his troubles to his Heavenly Father, and leaves them in His capable hands, knowing that His God is the good, loving, magnificent, powerful One who parceled out all heaven and earth. His trust is unwavering. He knows there's no situation beyond God's control, and he's willing to rest in that truth.

Think of it like this. God's the general. You're the foot soldier. God's in charge of where and how He needs you to serve Him. As you walk yielded to Him, He will guide and direct you. Then come what may—glory on the field of battle, or struggle and pain—you can trust Him to stick with you through thick and thin, equipping you and strengthening you every step of the way.

🗩 Engage

Paul risked prison time for THE Cause of spreading the gospel.

What are you willing to risk for THE Cause of Christ?

Awkwardness?
REJECTION?
Your Image?
Popularity?

Right now, get down on your knees and have a conversation with your magnificent Heavenly Father about what you're willing to risk for Him. Then take a risk today for the sake of the gospel and share the following video with a friend who needs to hear about Jesus: www.Lifein6Words.com.

Power Time

Ephesians 3:16-17a
I ask him to strengthen you by his Spirit—not a brute strength but a glorious inner strength—that Christ will live in you as you open the door and invite him in.

Explore

I come from a rough, tough, inner city family of body builders and thugs. Some of my uncles won body building titles and some did prison time for assault. Muscles were important. Brute strength was respected, even glorified.

My problem was that I didn't have the biceps that my other family members did. I was always more of a talker than a fighter. In the words of my Uncle Jack, I got my muscles in my jaw.

But I took comfort in a different kind of power. You see, **there's another kind of strength that's even more powerful and glorious than the abs of an award-winning body builder.**

It's the inner strength that flows forth when we yield to the work of the Holy Spirit in our lives, and tap into the spiritual power source that only He provides. That's what Paul's talking about here in his prayer for the church in Ephesus.

Sometimes, it helps me to visualize that I have an oversized power outlet in the middle of my chest that connects to the inner workings of my soul, sort of like Ironman. Then I visualize the Holy Spirit as a massive, never-ending power source—like a million suns times a billion stars. Scripture tells me that as a follower of Jesus, I can plug my soul into the incredible power source of the Holy Spirit—the same power source that raised Jesus from the dead (Philippians 3:10).

When I fail to plug into that power source, I struggle and flounder on my own as I try to live the Christian life in my own strength, through sheer determination and human willpower.

I'm doomed to fail on my own. I run out of juice in no time flat.

> BUT IF I **PLUG INTO THE POWER OF THE HOLY SPIRIT**, HE SUPPLIES ME WITH **"A GLORIOUS INNER STRENGTH"** THAT'S FREELY AVAILABLE TO THOSE WHO INVITE **CHRIST** INTO THEIR LIVES.

☀ Encounter

As we talked about in Devo #4, every Christian receives the Holy Spirit at the moment they first trust in Christ. But day-by-day, hour-by-hour, moment-by-moment, you and I must choose to continually walk in the power of the Spirit. If you choose to ignore Him, you can block this channel of strength in your life. But the more fully surrendered you are to Him, the more freely His power flows in you and through you.

Does this mean you'll never sin again, and you'll live a perfect, holy life? Unfortunately, no. As humans, we'll all continue to struggle with our impulses to be selfish, prideful, greedy, lust-filled and more. The important thing is that whenever you fall down, you confess your sin, ask forgiveness, pick yourself up in the power of the Holy Spirit and strive to live a life that is increasingly yielded to God.

🗨 Engage

One of my favorite verses about the power of the Holy Spirit at work in and through us is Acts 1:8 where Jesus says to His followers,

"But you will receive power when the Holy Spirit comes upon you. And you will be my witnesses, telling people about me everywhere—in Jerusalem, throughout Judea, in Samaria, and to the ends of the earth" (NLT).

Stop and pray right now, and invite the Holy Spirit to work in and through you during the coming day. Then take your cue from Acts 1:8, and think of another person you know who needs to hear Jesus' message of grace and hope. Ask the Spirit to use you to tell them about God's extravagant love for them.

Watch the one minute YouTube video found at the following link: www.somethingamazing. net/God. Then send your friend a text with the question "Do you believe in God?" and the link in it. Ask them to watch the video, and tell them you want to know what they think of it. Set up a time to get together to talk about what they think God is like. Ask them questions about what they believe, and share what you believe.

Immense

Ephesians 3:17b-19

And I ask him that with both feet planted firmly on love, you'll be able to take in with all followers of Jesus the extravagant dimensions of Christ's love. Reach out and experience the breadth! Test its length! Plumb the depths! Rise to the heights! Live full lives, full in the fullness of God.

 Explore

What's the biggest, hugest, most immense thing you can think of?

Some might look up at the night sky, see the expanse of stars

in our Milky Way, and say that it's the most massive thing they can think of—after all, our own sun is 93,000,000 miles away—and it's just the closest star among the 300 BILLION stars in our Milky Way galaxy.[2]

Or if you're a science nerd, you might suggest that the universe is the hugest, most massive thing in existence. By some estimates, the distance from here to the edge of the observable universe is 46 billion light years. Since one light year equals roughly six trillion miles (BTW, a light year is a unit of length, not time), that means 46,000,000,000 x 6,000,000,000,000 = ?????????.

Let's just say it's a whole bunch more than my puny calculator OR my puny brain can handle. But I'm pretty sure that if you want to head for the edge, you should probably pack a lunch.

☼ Encounter

Yet here in his prayer in Ephesians 3:18-19, Paul is reminding us that the very One who created the universe itself loves us with a love of *"extravagant dimensions." "Reach out and experience the breadth! Test its length! Plumb the depths! Rise to the heights! Live full lives, full in the fullness of God,"* he says.

The NLT translation puts it this way: *"May you experience the love of Christ, though it is too great to understand fully."* Like the massiveness of the universe itself—it's too wide and long, too deep and high for our puny brains to fully grasp. Yet, Scripture has much to tell us about God's *extravagant* love.

Perhaps the clearest display of this God-sized love can be found in one of the most well-known and well-loved verses in the entire Bible: *"For God loved the world so much that he gave his one and only Son, so that everyone who believes in him will not perish but have eternal life"* (John 3:16, NLT). God the Father sent His Son Jesus to be a sacrifice for our sins, because He'd rather die than live without you.

Engage

Over and over again, the Apostle Paul draws us back to the immensity and extravagance of Christ's love for us. Incessantly, he prods and prays that we would live in it more and more fully! Why? Because when we're filled with the fullness of God, God is able to work powerfully through us.

Close your eyes and visualize this immense love that wraps the entire universe in its arms.

Then crawl up in your *Abba*-Daddy's lap. Rest there in His love.

But don't keep this love to yourself, hidden behind an invisibility cloak. Pray and look for ways to share the immensity of God's love that's available through the cross of Christ with someone today.

Beyond Your Wildest Dreams

14

Ephesians 3:20

God can do anything, you know—far more than you could ever imagine or guess or request in your wildest dreams! He does it not by pushing us around but by working within us, his Spirit deeply and gently within us.

🧭 Explore

In your wildest dreams, what do you long for—popularity, romance, money, beauty, brains, fame, talent?

Well, let me tell you straight up—that's not exactly what today's verse in Ephesians 3 is talking about. God is not your own personal cosmic vending machine, or your butler in the sky.

No, today's *"in your wildest dreams"* faith-filled verse is the culmination of the Apostle Paul's prayer that started back in Ephesians 3:16. As we've unpacked his prayer over these last few days, we've taken bite-sized pieces, and explored what they mean, and how they might apply to your life. But now it's time to step back and look at Paul's prayer as a whole unit. And when you do that, you can see a logical progression.

The progression goes like this: As you yield your life to Jesus, He'll fill you with a glorious inner strength that's powered by the Holy Spirit, and you'll more and more fully experience God's infinite love and the fullness of a life lived with God at its very center.

And now, finally, in verse 20 today, you see the culminating outcome that bursts forth when you get serious about doing life with Jesus, and living in light of these spiritual truths: A life of radical impact. God will be able to do far more in and through you than you can imagine *"in your wildest dreams"* as *"His Spirit works deeply and gently"* within you.

☀ Encounter

Almost everyone wants to live a life of impact. Most people try to do this in their own human strength. They tap into their talent smarts, money, **power** or whateve live a **life** of influence and impact.

They network, play politics and continually repackage themselves to maximum advantage. Some do all this for their own selfish gain and personal ego boost. And some do it for the good of others (or at least, so they can feel better about themselves by being do-gooders).

But along comes Paul's prayer here, totally upending our self-focused mindset about how to live a successful, impacting life.

His prayer points us toward the secret to a life of

REAL
RADICAL
L A S T I N G
IMPACT

beyond our wildest dreams.

And here's the secret: A life of eternal impact bursts forth when we willingly yield our lives to Jesus, plug into the power of the Holy Spirit, and live in the fullness of God's lavish love for us, SO THAT He can work in us and through us to advance His kingdom, and bring glory to His name. After all, what could be more impacting than to introduce others to Jesus, and change the spiritual trajectory of their lives for all eternity?!?

pularity,
d strive to

Engage

A life yielded to Jesus doesn't mean that we give up our own personalities, or ignore our natural gifts and abilities—after all they are God-given gifts. But it does mean that we surrender them to God, and strive to use them in the power of the Holy Spirit for God's glory, not our own.

So, think through your own personal gifts and abilities.

Maybe you're good at *music*, SPORTS, writing, art, humor, serving others or something else.

Whatever it is for you, pick one area that rises to the top of your list.

Then spend some time in prayer surrendering that gift or ability to God. Tell Him you want to use it more and more fully for His glory, and not your own. Finally, think of at least one specific way you can use that particular talent or ability to bring God glory in the next day or two. For example, you might use it to help someone else for His sake, or to point someone toward Jesus. **Be creative!** But whatever you decide to do, just be sure you do something!

Love Like That!

Ephesians 5:1-2

Watch what God does, and then you do it, like children who learn proper behavior from their parents. Mostly what God does is love you. Keep company with him and learn a life of love. Observe how Christ loved us. His love was not cautious but extravagant. He didn't love in order to get something from us but to give everything of himself to us. Love like that.

Explore

Jesus was once asked to summarize God's most important command for us as His followers. Matthew 22:36-40 recounts the story like this:

"Teacher, which is the greatest commandment in the Law?"

Jesus replied: "'Love the Lord your God with all your heart and with all your soul and with all your mind.' This is the first and greatest commandment. And the second is like it: 'Love your neighbor as yourself.' All the Law and the Prophets hang on these two commandments" (NIV).

Love God. Love others.

Simple words, but impossible to live out in your own strength, right? Loving with the extravagant, self-sacrificing love of Christ only happens when you *"keep company with Him."* And then out of the rich and nurturing ground of your relationship with Him, your desire and ability to love others will grow and deepen, becoming less and less cautious, and more and more fearless.

☼ Encounter

So what does it look like in the nitty-gritty of your everyday life to *"keep company with him and learn a life of love"?* God's given us several amazing resources to help us!

Scripture says that doing life with Jesus works best when you...

- **...pray,** for this is your conversational connection to God. *"Never stop praying"* (1 Thessalonians 5:17, NLT).

- **...worship,** for no one can enter God's presence in true worship and not be changed. *"Shout with joy to the Lord, all the earth! Worship the Lord with gladness. Come before him, singing with joy"* (Psalm 100:1-2, NLT).

- **...stay** plugged into the power of the Holy Spirit, for He must breathe His power into everything you do. *"I pray that from his glorious, unlimited resources he will empower you with inner strength through his Spirit. Then Christ will make his home in your hearts as you trust in him. Your roots will grow down into God's love and keep you strong"* (Ephesians 3:16-17, NLT).

- **...read** God's Word, for it will take you deeper and deeper in your relationship with the Father, Son and Holy Spirit. *"All Scripture is inspired by God and is useful to teach us what is true and to make us realize what is wrong in our lives. It corrects us when we are wrong and teaches us to do what is right. God uses it to prepare and equip his people to do every good work"* (2 Timothy 3:16-17, NLT).

ENGAGED 15

- **...live in community** with other Christians, for they will love, encourage and help you walk with Jesus. *"Let the message about Christ, in all its richness, fill your lives. Teach and counsel each other with all the wisdom he gives. Sing psalms and hymns and spiritual songs to God with thankful hearts"* (Colossians 3:16, NLT).

- **...live and give Jesus' gospel message** of love **and forgiveness.** *"I pray that your partnership with us in the faith may be effective in deepening your understanding of every good thing we share for the sake of Christ."* (Philemon 1:6, NIV).

Engage

"Watch what God does, and then you do it... Keep company with him and learn a life of love... Love like that."

Learning a life of love doesn't happen overnight. You have to consistently tap into the resources that God's provided to help you.

How are you doing? Take a candid assessment.

Rate yourself on how effectively you're *"keeping company with Him"* in the six areas found on the following page. Note which are your strongest and your weakest.

"Keeping Company with Him" Self-Assessment

How are you doing?

PRAYER

```
1     2     3     4     5
```
WEAKER · · · STRONGER

WORSHIP

```
1     2     3     4     5
```
WEAKER · · · STRONGER

PLUGGING INTO THE POWER OF THE HOLY SPIRIT

```
1     2     3     4     5
```
WEAKER · · · STRONGER

BIBLE READING

```
1     2     3     4     5
```
WEAKER · · · STRONGER

HANGING WITH OTHER CHRISTIANS

```
1     2     3     4     5
```
WEAKER · · · STRONGER

SHARING THE GOSPEL

```
1     2     3     4     5
```
WEAKER · · · STRONGER

After you've assessed where you're at with each, thank God for your strongest area, and pray about your weakest one.

Ask God to meet you in your weakness, and begin to help you improve.

Then identify one thing you can do right away, so you can more consistently tap into that particular resource that can help you *"learn a life of love."*

Ask your youth leader for help with this if you can't come up with an idea on your own.

Dear God,

Because I want to *"keep company"* with you and *"learn a life of love,"* please help me make the following change in my life...

Live and Love Before a Watching World

16

Ephesians 5:3-4

Don't allow love to turn into lust, setting off a downhill slide into sexual promiscuity, filthy practices, or bullying greed. Though some tongues just love the taste of gossip, those who follow Jesus have better uses for language than that. Don't talk dirty or silly. That kind of talk doesn't fit our style. Thanksgiving is our dialect.

Explore

Lust, greed, gossip, foul language, coarse jokes—sounds like an honest description of what a typical American student is surrounded by on their school campuses day in and day out, doesn't it?

I went to a Christian school, and I'll never forget being shocked at the kinds of things some of the guys would joke about in the basketball locker room. Having been redeemed from a pretty sinful background, I was expecting more from the guys I went to Christian school with. But it shouldn't have surprised me. **Sin is all around us and a battle every Christian has to fight.**

The stark reality is that you and I inhabit a world where lust runs riot, porn is just a mouse click away, materialism is a measure of success, self-centeredness permeates the very air we breathe, gossip is bonding time with our friends and f-bombs fly like cannon fodder on a battlefield.

WHEN WE'RE SERIOUS ABOUT FOLLOWING JESUS, OUR LIVES BECOME A SPIRITUAL BATTLEFIELD.

All of us must continually, courageously do battle against what I call the Triple Threat: the world, the flesh and the devil.

1. **The world around us.** Lured by things like gossip, cheating and porn, we think... "Everybody's doing it, so why shouldn't I?"

2. **The flesh, our own appetites within.** Attracted by lust, addictions, selfishness and materialism we think... "I want what I want, even if it's wrong."

3. **The devil, who seeks to deceive us and damage our relationship with Jesus.** Bombarded by doubts, deception and despair, we think... "I'm so alone. God doesn't really love me. I'm sure I'll be more popular, or happy, or whatever, if I just..."

-Ö- Encounter

As Jesus followers, wallowing in sinful habits *"doesn't fit our style."* Sin creates "static" that messes with the intimacy of our relationship with God, and it damages our witness for Jesus before a watching world.

But the **Apostle Paul** points us to a better way, the way of *"thanksgiving."*

Say what?

Seriously, that's probably what you're thinking right now, isn't it? What in the world does thanksgiving have to do with battling sinful habits? Perhaps the NLT translation communicates this truth more clearly. It says: *"Instead, let there be thankfulness to God."*

Instead of sin, let there be thankfulness to God. It's a simple, yet life-changing truth.

It's easy to get weighed down and overwhelmed by your sin, and all the ways you don't measure up, if you're only thinking about all the "oughts" and "shoulds" of the Christian life. But if you focus on your thankfulness to God for all He's done for you, and continually remind yourself of His love and incredible sacrifice for you, your heart responds in gratitude. A heart of thanksgiving draws you close to Him, and makes you long to follow Him and serve Him, not because you "have to," but because you "want to."

Trust me, I've learned from experience that Paul's dead-on here! Duking it out with sin in the power of the Holy Spirit because you **WANT TO** follow Jesus out of gratitude to God, is always way more effective than leaning on your own willpower, guilt or fear.

ENGAGED 16

Engage

Yesterday, we looked at six God-given resources you can tap into as you *"keep company"* with Jesus and *"learn a life of love."* These same six resources will also help you battle the Triple Threat.

So right now, think about an area of sin that you've been struggling with. It could be lust, gossip, lying, selfishness, cheating, or any number of other possibilities. Pick the one that's pricking your conscious today.

Then take another look at the following list of six, but this time, consider how each of these can help you in your struggle with sin. Then pick one and do it today.

1. **PRAYER** – Ask God for help as you battle your sin.

2. **WORSHIP** – Focus on your thankfulness to God and His unconditional love for you.

3. **PLUGGING INTO THE POWER OF THE HOLY SPIRIT** – Yield yourself to the power of the Holy Spirit and tap into His strength when you're tempted.

4. **BIBLE READING** – Read Romans 7:15-25.

5. **HANGING WITH OTHER CHRISTIANS** – Ask a trusted Christian friend to pray for you and hold you accountable.

6. **SHARING THE GOSPEL** – The very act of sharing your faith stretches and grows you and helps you keep your focus on Jesus.

Don't Be a User

Ephesians 5:5

You can be sure that using people or religion or things just for what you can get out of them—the usual variations on idolatry—will get you nowhere, and certainly nowhere near the kingdom of Christ, the kingdom of God.

Explore

Have you ever been around a "user"? I'm not talking about drugs here. I'm talking about someone who sucks the life out of relationships as they selfishly use others for their own personal agenda. For example, they may be popularity addicts, drama queens/kings or perpetually insecure emotional sponges who use others to feed their own ego.

Here's an all too common example of how this plays out in just one dimension of teen life: sexual attraction. **God designed sex as a beautiful expression of love, commitment and intimacy between a man and woman in the context of a lifelong marriage relationship.** But "users" distort God's gift and see the world through the filter of lustful sexual attraction. From porn to friends with benefits, they turn what was intended as a selfless gift to one's spouse, into a selfish appetite to be satisfied here and now.

But our selfish impulses reach far beyond sexual attraction. They impact almost every aspect of our lives, from our desire for success, to our obsession with the latest tech toy or fashion trend. They push us to compete with others in unhealthy ways, and become our idols so that life becomes all about us and not all about God.

-☼- **Encounter**

In John 15:12, Jesus told His followers, *"This is my command: Love one another the way I loved you. This is the very best way to love."*

How can we love others like Christ loves us if we're viewing them through eyes of manipulation and are driven by our own selfish desires?

Philippians 2:3-7 shows us what selfless love looks like—

Don't be selfish; don't try to impress others. Be humble, thinking of others as better than yourselves. Don't look out only for your own interests, but take an interest in others, too.

You must have the same attitude that Christ Jesus had.
Though he was God,
he did not think of equality with God
as something to cling to.
Instead, he gave up his divine privileges;
he took the humble position of a slave
and was born as a human being (NLT).

Jesus was forgiving, self-sacrificing **and *unconditionally* loving—** the total opposite of being a user.

So as children of His kingdom, we must continually strive to love like He did, being quick to forgive, generous with others and unconditionally loving, even when they don't respond to our kindness the way we think they should.

ENGAGED 17

Engage

Don't be a user.

Be a giver.

Do something generous for someone in the next day or two. Be creative! As an extra challenge, consider directing your generosity toward someone you don't know very well (i.e., a loner at school), or someone you sometimes have relational challenges with (i.e., a sibling or a rival). Here are a few ideas to get you started, or you can come up with your own.

- Go for coffee or ice cream, your treat.
- Encourage someone with a handwritten note.
- Listen well.
- Offer to pray for someone.
- Help someone with their homework.
- Invite someone to lunch, your treat.
- Share the gospel.
- Give a compliment.
- _____
- _____

Hijacked?!?

Ephesians 5:6-7
Don't let yourselves get taken in by religious smooth talk. God gets furious with people who are full of religious sales talk but want nothing to do with him.

 Explore

Has Christianity been hijacked?

When non-Christians, ages 16 to 29, were asked to freely comment on their impressions of Christianity, one of the common responses was "Christianity in today's society no longer looks like Jesus."

As researchers drilled down more specifically about these young peoples' perceptions of Christianity, here are just a couple of the disturbing stats they uncovered:

87% **characterized Christians as judgmental.**

85% **characterized Christians as hypocritical.**[3]

Regardless of whether this is a fair or unfair description of Christians today, it's a shocking commentary on the effectiveness of our Christian witness to the unbelieving world!

The researchers noted that it was surprising how many of the respondents' negative perceptions of Christianity "were rooted in specific stories and personal interactions with Christians and in churches." It appears this negative view of Christianity is not just the result of the media bashing and trashing Christianity. These perceptions appear to be based on personal experience.

Which brings us to today's verses in Ephesians 5.

Don't let your Christianity get hijacked by *"religious smooth talk. God gets furious with people who are full of religious sales talk but want nothing to do with him."*

We would be wise to remember that Jesus reserved His harshest anger, not for the hookers and crooks He hung out with, but for the Pharisees, who were self-righteously distorting God's message of love into a burdensome list of rules and creating stumbling blocks to God (Matthew 23:23-32).

☀ Encounter

Which raises an important question: How can you, who've experienced God's grace, forgiveness, love and compassion, represent Him more authentically to those around you who so desperately need Him?

Do a character check, and prayfully ask God for His insight as you consider the following questions:

- **Are you personally judgmental?**

  Are you quick to act as judge and jury when a non-Christian behaves in ways your Christian faith identifies as sin? Remember Jesus' response to those whose lifestyle choices were contrary to the Law (John 4 and John 8:1-11). Approach others in a way that communicates that you're "just one beggar showing another beggar where to find bread."

- **Are you hypocritical?**

  A hypocrite is someone who is pretending to be something they are not. Someone who is not being real, but is playing a role to impress others. Are you genuine? Is what others see on the outside really who you are on the inside?

☀ Engage

Once you've had your character check conversation with God, continue the conversation with your friends who don't know Jesus personally. **Try asking them questions like:**

- What's your impression of Christianity? Is it positive or negative?

- Do you view Christians as judgmental? Hypocritical? Why or why not?

- And if you're really brave, ask your friends what they think of your Christian walk. Do they think you are judgmental or hypocritical? (Caution: Don't ask, if you aren't willing to hear the truth without getting defensive.)

While you may not feel like you're able to single-handedly change society's perception of Christianity, **you can, through God's grace and power, strive to become more like Jesus.** And then you can positively impact the impression everyone around you has of Christians... like the pebble in the pond, creating ever-increasing ripples, and eventually Christianity will begin to look more and more like Jesus. It can start with you!

Carpe Diem 19

Ephesians 5:8-10

You groped your way through that murk once, but no longer. You're out in the open now. The bright light of Christ makes your way plain. So no more stumbling around. Get on with it! The good, the right, the true—these are the actions appropriate for daylight hours. Figure out what will please Christ, and then do it.

🧭 Explore

Carpe diem. Seize the day!

"No more stumbling around. Get on with it!... Figure out what will please Christ, and then do it."

I'll never forget the lengths I would go to in high school to get that "one girl" to say YES and go out with me. I was head over heels in (puppy?) love with her, and I would do anything to make her happy.

She was a cowgirl, and rode horses in the rodeo. I was a city boy, and drove fast cars on asphalt. But when this cowgirl batted her long eyelashes and asked me for some help, I didn't hesitate. Soon this city boy had a shovel in his hand, and was moving a **SEVEN FOOT TALL PILE OF HORSE MANURE.**

Love spills over into a "whatever it takes" attitude of gratitude that is more than willing to step in it or shovel it because of love.

The same is true of our relationship with God. When we are convinced He loves us, then we are willing to do anything and everything in response to His love.

WHAT DOES THIS LOOK LIKE? WALKING IN HIS LIGHT. GROWING IN CHRISTLIKENESS. BECOMING MORE AND MORE LIKE HIM.

In your efforts to become more and more like Him, it helps to take a look at the big picture of what Jesus was all about when He walked this earth.

First, He was definitely about His relationship with His heavenly Father. **He lived a sinless life of total surrender and dependence on His Father.** Secondly, He was also about His mission. He was the Son of God, and He came to earth to save us—to make a way for us to have a restored relationship with God by dying on the cross as an atonement for our sins.

☀ Encounter

Jesus was on a desperate search and rescue mission for the lost. It was a passion and focus of His life—it was His cause.

The amazing thing is that Jesus has invited you to join Him in His cause of reaching the lost. Listen to His words again in John 2:22, *"As the Father has sent me, so I am sending you."* And right before He ascended into heaven in Matthew 28:19, He commanded His followers to *"go and make disciples."*

So if you want to become more and more like Jesus, you too must nurture the twofold focus of your spiritual walk: growing deep in your personal relationship with God, AND joining Jesus in His Cause of reaching the lost.

ENGAGED 19

⌨ Engage

The very fact that you are reading Day 19 of this devotional book tells me that you are already pretty serious about growing in your relationship God. The bigger challenge for most students is the second part about becoming more like Jesus when it comes to reaching the lost. So let's focus on that one right now. After all, our verse today says, *"Get on with it!... Figure out what will please Christ, and then do it."*

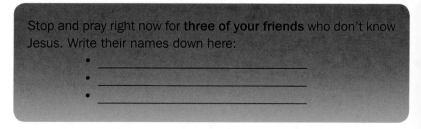

Stop and pray right now for **three of your friends** who don't know Jesus. Write their names down here:

- _____
- _____
- _____

Then seize the day and step out for THE Cause of Christ! Find a way to initiate a conversation about God with one person today—it could be face-to-face, online, on the phone or wherever. Here are a few ideas that might help you bring God up in your conversation, or come up with your own approach.

- Share the YouTube video found at www.somethingamazing.net/God.

- Share the YouTube video found at www.somethingamazing.net/then-what.

- Share the website www.Lifein6Words.com.

- Share the website www.somethingamazing.net.

Carpe diem! Make it happen today!

Out of Your Coffin!

Ephesians 5: 11-17

Don't waste your time on useless work, mere busywork, the barren pursuits of darkness. Expose these things for the sham they are. It's a scandal when people waste their lives on things they must do in the darkness where no one will see. Rip the cover off those frauds and see how attractive they look in the light of Christ.

Wake up from your sleep,

Climb out of your coffins;

Christ will show you the light!

So watch your step. Use your head. Make the most of every chance you get. These are desperate times! Don't live carelessly, unthinkingly. Make sure you understand what the Master wants.

⊘ Explore

Remember Gandalf's wise words in *The Fellowship of the Ring*? **"All we have to decide is what to do with the time that is given us."**

If you've ever been at a cemetery for the graveside burial of a loved one, you know that nothing represents the finality of physical death more starkly than the sight of the coffin at the gravesite.

So imagine with me for a moment, that your physical life has come to an end, and you're the one lying in the coffin.

And **now,** *you and Jesus are looking back over the movie of your life, reviewing* **how you** *spent the days He gave you on this earth.*

It's a sobering thought, isn't it?

Hopefully, there would be plenty of instances where your life was packed and stacked with service to Christ and His Cause. But would there also be all too many hours and hours of trivial, useless time wasters and *"barren pursuits of darkness"* exposed by *"the light of Christ"*?

☼ Encounter

Which brings urgency to the Apostle Paul's words today in Ephesians 5 when he tells you to climb out of your coffin and step into the light of Christ: *"Don't waste your time on useless work, mere busywork, the barren pursuits of darkness...It's a scandal when people waste their lives...Use your head. Make the most of every chance you get. These are desperate times! Don't live carelessly, unthinkingly. Make sure you understand what the Master wants."*

Now consider this. Millennials—young people ages 14 to 29—spend 17.8 hours engaged in media daily. Obviously some of these hours are overlapping, due to young people's mad multitasking abilities to surf the net, listen to music and text all at the same time. "Web surfing, along with social media activities and smartphone interactions such as texting and chatting take up the biggest chunk of their media time daily, claiming fully 50% of the total."[4]

🗨 Engage

Are all these hours spent engaged in media, day in and day out, a waste of time? Not necessarily, if they're genuinely helping you build relationships with others that are meaningful and Christ-honoring. But if you're a typical Christian student, there are no doubt some things you can do to make your media presence and usage more God-honoring and gospel-advancing.

ENGAGED 20

So think about your media habits, and ask yourself some tough questions about whether you're spending too much of your time *"carelessly and unthinkingly"* in pointless, *"barren pursuits."*

Here are a few questions to get you started. But since you know your own media habits best, feel free to add your own probing questions to the list…

- Does your online profile clearly communicate that you are a follower of Jesus? Should it?

- Do your "likes" reflect the things you think Jesus would like too?

- Do you ever text or post links to videos and music that help initiate spiritual conversations or point others toward Jesus?

- Does any of your online behavior clearly bring discredit to Jesus?

- Have you ever shared your faith in a gaming room or chat room?

- _____

- _____

- _____

Then climb out of your "coffin," so to speak, and make the most of the time you've been given! Do at least one thing today online or on your phone that will help you initiate a spiritual conversation with a friend who needs Jesus.

Drinking Songs

Ephesians 5:18-20

Don't drink too much wine. That cheapens your life. Drink the Spirit of God, huge draughts of him. Sing hymns instead of drinking songs! Sing songs from your heart to Christ. Sing praises over everything, any excuse for a song to God the Father in the name of our Master, Jesus Christ.

⊘ Explore

The more things change, the more they stay the same... The same issue Paul is tackling head on here, still wreaks havoc in the lives of all too many people today: alcohol.

In 2013, **22.1% of high school seniors surveyed reported that they binge drink** (defined as 5 or more drinks in a row in the past 2 weeks).[5] And the problem only escalates as teenagers head off to college—40% of college students surveyed indicate that they binge drink.[6] The toll for this kind of alcohol abuse is devastating, from drunk driving to date rape to life-long alcohol addiction, the fallout is toxic.

Paul had it right when he cautioned that too much drinking *"cheapens your life."* But isn't his alternative intriguing — or perhaps we might even say — shocking?

This isn't the first time Scripture talks about drunkenness and being filled with the Holy Spirit in the same breath. On the very Day of Pentecost—the day the Holy Spirit first roared into the Upper Room in Acts 2 and infused the early believers with His power—the onlookers actually accused those very first Spirit-filled Christians of being drunk!

Yield your life to the power of the Spirit of God

☀ Encounter

So why the comparison? Think of it this way. Too much alcohol will sweep through your system, and influence your personality, judgment, behavior and your very perception of the world around you. And so does plugging into the power of the Holy Spirit! When you yield your life to the power of the Spirit of God, He sweeps in and influences all these same things about you. Galatians 5:22-23 describes the impact of Spirit in our lives this way:

He brings gifts into our lives, much the same way that fruit appears in an orchard—things like affection for others, exuberance about life, serenity. We develop a willingness to stick with things, a sense of compassion in the heart, and a conviction that a basic holiness permeates things and people. We find ourselves involved in loyal commitments, not needing to force our way in life, able to marshal and direct our energies wisely.

WHEN YOU **DRINK IN** HUGE **DRAUGHTS OF THE HOLY SPIRIT**, **INSTEAD** OF DRINKING SONGS, YOU'LL BE SINGING **SONGS OF JOY** TO YOUR **GRACE-GIVING GOD!**

🗨 **Engage**

Remember, like we talked about in Devo #12, **plugging into the power of the Holy Spirit** is an ongoing process. It's something we must choose to do over and over.

So stop and pray right now, and ask the Spirit to do His work in and through you today.

Next, go find a recording of your favorite Christian song. Listen to it two or three times throughout your day. As you do, zero in on a line or two that particularly speak to you and helps you lift your heart to God in praise and worship.

Then pray it

from your heart

to God's heart.

Strength Training 22

Ephesians 6:10-13 (NIV)

Finally, be strong in the Lord and in his mighty power. Put on the full armor of God, so that you can take your stand against the devil's schemes. For our struggle is not against flesh and blood, but against the rulers, against the authorities, against the powers of this dark world and against the spiritual forces of evil in the heavenly realms. Therefore put on the full armor of God, so that when the day of evil comes, you may be able to stand your ground, and after you have done everything, to stand.

🧭 Explore

Scripture is crystal clear that there's a spiritual battle being waged between the forces of good and the forces of evil. You can see the collateral damage of this battle all around you, if you look. Evil run amok—cruelty, rape, injustice, bullying, gossip, lying, jealousy, people hurting people.

Since the Garden of Eden, the evil one and his dark army of fallen angels have been out to destroy us humans—and not just on some grand, impersonal, cosmic level. These dark forces seek to destroy you, too—you personally.

You ignore this spiritual reality at your own peril. Why do I say that?

Because if you try to live the Christian life oblivious to Satan and his dark army, you'll be continually tempted to live in your own strength, trying to fight your own spiritual battles, rather than tapping into the Lord's mighty power, and putting on the spiritual armor He's provided you.

☀ Encounter

The Christian life is not a self-help exercise with three simple steps to a better life. If you're a committed follower of Jesus, you're walking around with a target on your back—and Satan and his forces of evil are taking aim. If they can't destroy you, they will, at the very least, try to deceive, distract and discourage you.

HOW?

Deception might look like...

a whisper in your ear that says, "God doesn't really love you. In fact, this grace-giving God Jesus talked about is simply too good to be true. Why not just dump this whole Jesus thing and get on with your life and do your own thing."

Distraction might look like...

sports, relationships, studies, gadgets, media—anything and everything—that might keep you so busy that you forget to put Jesus at the center of it all.

Discouragement might look like... a whisper in your ear that says, "God could never forgive you for that sin. You'll never measure up. You're worthless. God's disgusted with you, so you're in this alone. He's not going to help you with anything. Time to stress out, cuz it's all up to you to get your act together and build a "successful life," and you know you'll never be able to do that. You're such a loser."

EMBOLDENED 22

🗨 Engage

It's only in God's strength and power that you'll be able to consistently, successfully stand up to the evil one's schemes to deceive, distract and discourage. And that's why God's given you the armor you need to take a stand and fight back.

We'll be taking a look at these individual pieces of the spiritual armor God's provided you in the coming days, so stay tuned. But for today, spend some time thinking about which of the evil one's tactics you are personally most vulnerable to. Then have a conversation with God about it.

Deception

Distraction

Discouragement

Doubt and Guilt: Send 'em Running for the Hills

23

Ephesians 6:14 (NIV)

Stand firm then, with the belt of truth buckled around your waist, with the breastplate of righteousness in place...

Explore

"I get so confused sometimes, I'm not really sure what I believe is actually true about God."

"Sometimes I feel so guilty when I think about God. I'm sure He's so mad at me for all the bad stuff I've done, that He'll never forgive me."

Do doubts about truth with a capital "T" or questions about your right standing with God ever echo around inside your head? If so, you're not alone. I've talked to many Christian students who struggle with doubt and guilt.

At the Dare 2 Share conferences, **I get the privilege of ministering to thousands of teenagers from all across the nation. One thing that many of them have in common is DOUBT and GUILT.** I've talked to guys who felt guilty about sinful habits that they wrestle with, or girls who were confused about whether or not they were really saved because of things that they've done.

Fortunately, Paul lays out two pieces of armor that are designed to help you send these twin taunt-ers running for the hills: truth and righteousness. And the beautiful thing is that both of your mighty weapons against these twin scourges that plague many Christians drive you straight back to Jesus and His amazing love for you.

In John 14:6, Jesus said, *"I am the way and the truth and the life. No one comes to the Father except through me"* (NIV). Jesus is the belt of truth you can buckle around your waist and trust in as you lean your life on Him and walk in His truth.

☀ Encounter

Am I saying here that you should never ask sincere questions about your faith? Not at all. Asking honest questions is what helps you make your faith your own, and not just something handed down from your parents or youth leader. The key when asking questions about God is to follow the truth wherever it leads, because when you do that, I'm confident it will always lead you to Jesus.

1 JOHN 5:20 EXPLAINS IT LIKE THIS: *And we know that the Son of God came so we could recognize and understand the truth of God—what a gift!—and we are living in the Truth itself, in God's Son, Jesus Christ. This Jesus is both True God and Real Life.*

And instead of succumbing to an unending stream of guilt and blame, Paul offers another piece of armor for your defense, the righteousness of Christ. Let's face it. We are all guilty, imperfect sinners who fall abysmally short of God's holiness. But the good news of the gospel that you can hold up to protect your heart against the evil one's flaming arrows is this: *"For God made Christ, who never sinned, to be the offering for our sin, so that we could be made right with God through Christ"* (2 Corinthians 5:21, NLT).

Your **right standing** with God doesn't come from **your own human efforts.**

You could never be good enough to earn your way into heaven. That would be like trying to swim from California to Hawaii. It's too far. It's not humanly possible. Same thing with trying to earn your way to heaven. It's not up to you. You can't do it, but Jesus did it for you. So you can stand on His atoning work on the cross when He died for you. Your sins are forgiven—past, present and future.

The cross of Christ is absolutely the only possible source of your right standing before God, both back when you first put your faith and trust in Jesus, but also now, as you walk the road as His follower and continue to miss the mark.

EMBOLDENED 23

Engage

Do you have any unsettling questions about God and your relationship with Him that have been knocking around inside your head for awhile? If so, take a minute and write the most pressing one down.

Start by having a conversation with God about it. Then approach a trusted adult, tell them about your assignment today, explain your question and ask them to help you explore it—this could be a parent, youth leader, pastor or mentor.

Let's Roll!

...And with your feet fitted with the readiness that comes from the gospel of peace.

🧭 Explore

Imagine you got up on the morning of your 16th birthday, and your parents took you outside and presented you with the keys to a shiny new Camaro. That would be amazingly incredible good news, wouldn't it?! You might even think you'd died and gone to heaven! Your very own awesome wheels—you'd be ready to roll whenever and wherever you wanted. And you'd want to tell everyone you knew all about it! You'd probably even be eager to take them along for a spin.

I'll never forget when I got to drive a sweet Camaro from Colorado to California for my boss. (Yes, I got paid to do it!!) Although I was a teenager, I had at my command an engine with unimaginable horsepower and torque. While I didn't actually understand what those two words meant, I did know that it could drive FAST!

As much as you and I might enjoy driving down the road in a shiny Camaro, the reality is that if you're a follower of Jesus, you've been given something **even more spectacular** to travel through life with—the perfect peace with God that comes from the message of the gospel.

The gospel is an essential piece of your spiritual armor, for it gives you the steady, unwavering peace you need on your journey through life, especially when storms are swirling all around you and the evil one is tempting you to doubt God's goodness. The gospel assures you of God's lavish love for you as His child.

☀ Encounter

The word "gospel" actually means "good news." It serves as part of your armor against the attacks of the evil one. But did you notice that when Paul introduces this piece of armor, it comes with a sense of movement, of action? Why do you think that is? I think it's because it's news too good to keep to yourself!

Are you ready to roll with the gospel? Are you ready to tell your friends about it, and introduce them to Jesus so they, too, can experience peace with God?

If you've never lead anyone else to faith in Jesus, let me tell you that it is the very best feeling in the whole world. Sure, bringing God up in conversation and sharing your faith can be awkward, scary and sometimes risky. But it's the best news on the planet, so it's worth the risk!

Plus, each time you explain the gospel of peace to someone, it reminds you of its magnificent power and presence in your own life. In Romans 1:16, Paul declares that the gospel is the very "power of God." Check it out: *"For I am not ashamed of the gospel, because it is the power of God that brings salvation to everyone who believes"* (NIV). In the original language of the New Testament—Greek—the word for "power" here is *dunamis*, from which we get our word dynamite! How is the gospel like **dynamite?** Because it can reach into the deepest part of someone's soul, and instantly blast them out of darkness into His MARVELOUS LIGHT!

Remember, whenever you share the gospel with someone, it's not the fancy words you say, or the compelling debating points you bring to the conversation. It's the *dunamis* power of the very gospel itself that impacts a soul!

Engage

Take a risk today. Share the gospel with at least one person— friend, stranger, whoever God lays on your heart. Pray for them, pray for courage, pray for the power of the gospel to pierce their heart. Then go do it.

LET'S ROLL!!!

Gear Up

25

Ephesians 6:16-17 (NIV)

In addition to all this, take up the shield of faith, with which you can extinguish all the flaming arrows of the evil one. Take the helmet of salvation and the sword of the Spirit, which is the word of God.

🧭 Explore

Fire will not be ignored. Believe me, I know from firsthand experience. When my car engine ignited in flames (no, not the Camaro I drove for my boss to Cali), I did not ignore it, because the fire was more than a minor distraction, it was a mortal danger!

Perhaps that's why Paul uses the symbolism of fire to describe the devastating impact the evil one's attacks can have when you fail to gear up.

Satan's and his minions' flaming arrows come in a wide range of shapes and sizes, **and they're usually custom-designed just especially for you and your particular weaknesses—the chinks in *your* armor.**

But consider this, all temptations—from lying to envy to sexual sin and more—basically derive from one central weakness that is common to all of mankind: doubting God's love and truth. It started clear back in the Garden of Eden, when Satan first tempted Adam and Eve to doubt God's love for them and question the truth of what He'd told them. And that very same root temptation shadows us every day of our lives.

☀ Encounter

Think through a few examples with me...

WHY
are we
tempted
TO LIE?

Basically, I think it's because we doubt God will take care of us, so we feel we need to take the situation into our own hands. Or we doubt we're loved unconditionally by God, so we seek the approval others so desperately that we feel compelled to lie to enhance our image or change our reality.

WHY do we BATTLE emotions like ENVY & GREED?

At their root, I believe it's because we don't fully embrace and lean our lives on God's love and goodness. We question why He hasn't seen fit to give us the material possessions, beauty, talent, or whatever we scramble about for. So we wallow in the ugly stench of our own selfishness.

WHY do we STRUGGLE with sexual sin?

Our battles with lust, porn, premarital sex and such are the results of our failure to stay firmly centered on the goodness and truth of God's blueprint for sexuality—which is sex between a man and a woman in the context of a committed, lifelong marriage. So we seek self-pleasure in all the wrong places, rather than trusting that God's ways are best for our body, mind and spirit.

But whatever flaming arrows of temptation the evil one sends your way, **gear up these three pieces of armor: faith, salvation and the Spirit-inspired Word of God.** For your faith and salvation will remind you of God's lavish love for you, and His goodness in sending Jesus to provide a way back to Him. And the Spirit and the Word will reveal at deeper and deeper levels, the truth of His character, love, purposes and plans for you as a follower of Jesus.

EMBOLDENED 25

🗨️ Engage

Staying grounded in God's great love and unshakable truth will motivate and strengthen you to battle every kind of temptation, so gear up with your weapons of faith, salvation and the Word of God.

When the evil one sends his flaming arrows your way, remember...

- **You've received new birth, a living hope and a heavenly inheritance.** *"Praise be to the God and Father of our Lord Jesus Christ! In his great mercy he has given us new birth into a living hope through the resurrection of Jesus Christ from the dead, and into an inheritance that can never perish, spoil or fade..."* (1 Peter 1:3-4a, NIV).

- **You're a child of God.** *"Yet to all who received him, to those who believed in his name, he gave the right to become children of God."* (John 1:12, NIV).

- **You're a new creation.** *"Therefore, if anyone is in Christ, that person is a new creation; the old has gone, the new is here!"* (2 Corinthians 5:17, NIV).

- **You're safe in God's love, no matter what comes your way.** *"For I am convinced that neither death nor life, neither angels nor demons, neither the present nor the future, nor any powers, neither height nor depth, nor anything else in all creation, will be able to separate us from the love of God that is in Christ Jesus our Lord."* (Romans 8:38-39, NIV).

Have a private talk with God about how more fully leaning your life on these truths might help you shore up the chinks in your armor.

Your Dusty Bazooka

26

Ephesians 6:18a

And pray in the Spirit on all occasions with all kinds of prayers and requests...

⊘ Explore

There it sets, unused and collecting dust. Although it is in good working condition, few think to use it.

What is the dusty bazooka hidden in your closet? It's prayer.

When the enemy bombards you with a barrage of temptations and doubts, and you're tempted to hunker in your bunker, quivering from fear, maybe your response is like mine was back when I was a teenager. I threw snowballs and pebbles. And my paltry efforts bounced off of the Prince of Darkness and his army of fallen angels like Nerf pellets fired from a kid's toy gun.

Satan and his legions laughed and kept shooting to kill.

It was only when I learned to reach into my closet and pull out **the weapon called prayer** that the enemy began to *quiver in fear.*

☀ Encounter

The evil one is not afraid of your good intentions to live for Jesus and share your faith. But he is absolutely terrified of your sincere prayer—that underutilized and underestimated weapon at your daily disposal.

Looking back, if I were to single out one area of my life that I wish I'd taken more seriously as a Christian teenager, it's prayer! In every circumstance of life—in both the dreams and the disasters—it's THE game changer.

As the Apostle Paul remind us, *"For though we live in the world, we do not wage war as the world does. The weapons we fight with are not the weapons of the world. On the contrary, they have divine power to demolish strongholds"* (2 Corinthians 10:3-4, NIV).

When he **attacks**,
take aim and fire.

When he **tempts** you,
TAKE AIM AND FIRE.

When he tries to **discourage** you,
take aim and fire.

When you feel **intimidated** about sharing your faith,

TAKE AIM AND FIRE.

Prayer is our instant communication channel to the God of the Universe. It does much more than decimate our dangerous enemy. It encourages our soul, replenishes our hearts, builds up our fellow brothers and sisters in Christ and provides for our needs. It's the portal for praise, worship and thanksgiving toward God. Prayer does many things and all of them are good for our soul.

Engage

Dear Father,

Humbly, I come to you, so grateful to know that I can bring my cares and concerns to you anytime, anywhere, by simply pausing and talking to you. Right now, I want to talk to you about...

OMG! What Should I Say?

Ephesians 6:19 (NIV)

Pray also for me, that whenever I speak, words may be given me so that I will fearlessly make known the mystery of the gospel...

Explore

I remember the first time that I shared my faith. It was with five or six teenagers at Sloan's Lake in Denver. They were just standing around, so I walked up to them and started asking them questions.

Pretty soon we were in a conversation about spiritual things and soon after I was explaining the gospel to them the best that I knew how.

I was 10 years old at the time.

That may sound weird, a fifth grader sharing Jesus with a bunch of high school kids out of the blue. Was I scared? You bet. But really, I couldn't help myself. I had a passion to share the good news, so I prayed for opportunities, I prayed for boldness, and then I jumped in and did it.

☀ Encounter

Many students are fearful that they won't know what to say if they try to talk about Jesus with their friends. But just like the Apostle Paul, the antidote to your fear is prayer. Know that it's OK to face every opportunity you have to bring God up in conversation as an OMG moment—literally. Whenever your heart beats faster and your palms get sweaty as you seek to share your faith, launch into a short, silent "Oh, my God! Help!" prayer. Pray for the courage and the words you need to *"fearlessly make known the mystery of the gospel."*

I've also found that having a solid understanding from Scripture about your God-given authority to share the gospel with others can help us face down our faith-sharing fears.

As you read each of the following verses, pull out your bazooka—prayer—and finish the sentence that follows it, based on what you think this should look like in your own life.

1 Thessalonians 2:4a *"For we speak as messengers approved by God to be entrusted with the Good News. Our purpose is to please God, not people..."* (NLT).

Father God, I know you want me to carry Jesus' message of hope and grace to those around me, but sometimes I hesitate. Please help me... _____

_____

2 Timothy 1:7-8a *"For God has not given us a spirit of fear and timidity, but of power, love, and self-discipline. So never be ashamed to tell others about our Lord..."* (NLT).

God, thanks for the assurance that you've already equipped me with a spirit of *"power, love and self-discipline."* Help me tap into the power of your Holy Spirit at work within me and through me as I step out today and live in this truth by boldly...

🗩 Engage

Sharing your faith doesn't have to be a boot-quaking experience. There are lots of ways to bring God up in our conversations with your friends. Here are a few examples...

- Have you ever wondered about God?

- Would you mind telling me what's most important to you in the whole world?

- Where are you at when it comes to God and religion?

- Why do you think bad stuff happens? Why is the world so messed up?

- Where do you turn when people let you down or hurt you?

And if you have friends who are coming from a particular religion or worldview, check out **www.dare2share.org/ worldviews.** You'll find loads more faith sharing questions, compliments and insights there for thirteen diverse, distinct worldviews.

So pray for courage, equip yourself with the GOSPEL acrostic found on page 38, remember to **Ask-Admire-Admit** like we talked about on page 41, pick one of these opening questions, then try it out today on a friend who needs Jesus. Text them, call them, or do a face-to-face... just find a way to bring up God up in a conversation and look for an opening to talk about the gospel!

Fearless! Come What May... 28

Ephesians 6:19b-20

...that I will fearlessly make known the mystery of the gospel, for which I am an ambassador in chains. Pray that I may declare it fearlessly, as I should.

 Explore

Have you ever wondered what it would be like to be someone influential—like the President of the United States, or the billionaire Bill Gates, or the Ambassador to China?

Well, I've got news for you! You are someone influential!

Why do I say that? Because every single follower of Jesus has been given an awesome and fearsome privilege: *"We are Christ's ambassadors; God is making his appeal through us. We speak for Christ when we plead, "Come back to God!"* (2 Corinthians 5:20, NLT).

You are Christ's ambassador! You speak for Christ when you plead with your friends to *"Come back to God!"* And believe me, being Christ's ambassador is waaaaaaaaay more important that being the Ambassador to China, because it carries eternal significance.

☀ Encounter

When you *really* think about it, nothing else in this world compares to sharing Jesus' message of hope and life—eternal destinies hang in the balance! And Jesus has entrusted it to you and me! You've been given the privilege of passing His message on, by reaching out to those in your circle of influence with His good news of love, forgiveness and salvation.

Sharing Jesus' message with others is the most impacting thing you will ever, ever do. Introducing someone to Jesus is more life changing than winning the lottery. It's more world transforming than finding the cure to cancer. It's better than giving away a million dollars to some worthy cause. Because sharing Jesus with those who don't know Him can change someone's life at the deepest level—both now and for all eternity. And nothing else you could ever be involved in is more significant than that!

That's why we need to fearless!

☐ Engage

There's a simple tool called THE Cause Circle that can help you be more deliberate, purposeful and fearless about sharing the Good News with your friends. It helps you identify the friends you're going to pray for with passion, pursue with love and persuade with the truth of Jesus' gospel message.

THE Cause Circle...Making Disciples Who Make Disciples

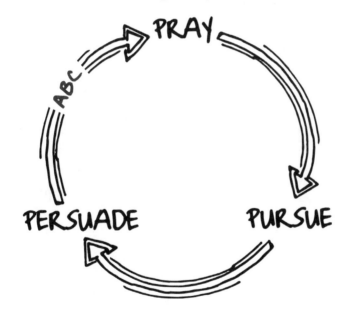

Start by writing the names of a few of your friends you want to introduce to Jesus in the center of the circle. Then Pray-Pursue-Persuade...

PRAY WITH PASSION. Ask God to prepare their hearts for His gospel message, and to provide you with courage, boldness and wisdom as you share your faith. The Apostle Paul was one brave, committed dude. He endured beatings, shipwreck, starvation, prison and more for the sake of the gospel. But even he knew that his efforts needed to be grounded in prayer so that he would be fearless and bold about sharing Jesus' message. How much more do you and I need to pray, pray, pray that we will be fearless for the sake of the gospel?

PURSUE WITH LOVE. Remember God's extravagant love for you! Then begin to pursue your friends with that same kind of generous, self-sacrificing love that comes from your relationship with Christ. Begin to be purposeful about weaving spiritual topics into your conversations. Ask questions, listen, or simply bring God up in conversation.

PERSUADE WITH TRUTH. Don't be afraid to persuade! The Greek word for persuade is used eight different times in the New Testament in direct connection with evangelism. This is not a used car salesman-type pitch, but a sincere, yet convincing appeal to the heart and mind of the unbeliever.

But Jesus calls us to be about more than just bringing people to a decision point of trusting in Him—though that's incredibly important. Remember in Matthew 28:19-20, He commands us to make disciples. So here are the three actions we're persuading our friends to embrace—these are the ABC's of becoming a disciple:

A **ccept Jesus** so they can live in the embrace of His fierce love.

B **elong to a church** so they can grow in their understanding of their wealth and walk in Christ.

C **ommit to THE Cause.** So they can, in turn, make disciples who make disciples.

So encircled by the lavish love of your heavenly Father, empowered by the Spirit, engaged in a life of love, and emboldened to fearlessly stand and be counted, go! Immerse yourself in prayer, then go out into your world each and every day, and boldly, fearlessly share Jesus' message of grace!

Because of God's great love for you, live a life that unleashes His fierce, extravagant love in your world!

EMBOLDENED 28

Endnotes

[1]Nasa Goddard Space Flight Center, "Nasa's Imagine the Universe!," Ask an Astrophysicist, http://imagine.gsfc.nasa.gov/docs/ask_astro/answers/021127a.html.

[2]Wikipedia, "Universe," http://en.wikipedia.org/wiki/Universe#Size.2C_age.2C_contents.2C_structure.2C_and_laws.

[3]Kinnsmsn, David, UnChristian (Grand Rapids, MI: Baker Books, 2007), page 28.

[4]Focus on the Family's Plugged In, The 18-Hour Media Day, April 7, 2014, https://connect.focusonthefamily.com/aprimo/OutboundMessage.aspx?O=a7167b0d32017bc88ece7a3897378337&T=b-333208886639fd5&D=b9ca57b2fbe8cb424588078533879 83f6a0f6be5ccdab113&M=b333208886639fd5&MSGID=8f-c3b56d344787bba9013c3d527d34c5d6d622040d3cfd-c2&A=4ae4442918c0c44fec6c6bf73e575cf6&l=4e338b695c08d8bf-12090415d9806177&S=50bafa8247c2c9775202820e18fc861d.

[5]NIH National Institute of Drug Abuse, Drug Facts: High School and Youth Trends, January 2014, http://www.drugabuse.gov/publications/drugfacts/high-school-youth-trends.

[6]US Department of Health and Human Services, "Results from the 2012 National Survey on Drug Use and Health: Summary of National Findings," Binge Alcohol Use among Adults Aged 18 to 22, by College Enrollment: 2002-2012, http://www.samhsa.gov/data/NSDUH/2012SummNatFindDetTables/NationalFindings/NSDUHresults2012.htm#ch3.1.6.